The Blog-Fire Power Blogging Method

Secrets That Only Pro-Bloggers Know, From Picking a Platform to Getting Paid

By Angela Atkinson

OnlineWritingPro.com| GoAskAngie.com | QueenBeeing.com

A BlissFire Media Production

Table of Contents

Introduction

So, I'm one of those creative types, and yeah, I might get a little off-track at times with all of my crazy ideas and project planning.

But when it comes down to it, I know how to get things done, and that's how I manage to do all the various projects, such as running several successful blogs and writing books (and how I am learning that I have to pick and choose carefully!).

Am I an overachiever? No. Hell no. I just do what I do and it works because I love it, because I am passionate about it and because to me, it does not feel like work - it feels a lot like doing something I love.

Truth is that even the most experienced and successful creative achievers can use a little help getting motivated to break out of the little box society has put them in and take a leap of faith into following their true passions.

For me, it's all about the writing, the understanding and the sharing of useful, touching, important or otherwise interesting and/or entertaining information. For me, it's who I am.

I've been making money with my blogs since 2005. I've probably made literally almost every dumb mistake a newbie could make, and I've done a lot of things right.

This book compiles the knowledge that I've learned which is relevant to today's blogger - everything that you need to know to build, manage and market a successful blog - a passion project of your very own - that can help you make money to support yourself and your family.

It won't be just sitting around in your PJs and playing on the internet for a few hours here and there - it'll be an ongoing, part-to-full-time job, if you want to make it work. But if you're following your passion, you're putting yourself in a whole new category: someone who does what they love and gets paid for it. For me, that's a lot like playing - like old adage says - if you love what you do, you'll never work a day in your life. If you want to get paid to blog about what you love, this book is for you. You'll get a step-by-step insider's look into what really works (and what doesn't) when it comes to blogging for profit.

Anyone can become a highly successful blogger, even you. Here is a blueprint on exactly what you need to do to make it happen.

The Blog-Fire Method Passion Project

They say that "follow your passion" is bad advice And maybe they're right. But the way I see it, being happy is what ultimately leads to having the abundant blessings we all want in life. And for me, that means following my passion.

As a result of my decade of blogging and of coaching business owners, writers, entrepreneurs and other professionals, I know something that you might not: almost ANYTHING can become fodder for a high-income-potential blog.

That means that almost anyone could feasibly make a living with their blog. That is the simple basis of the Blog-Fire Method - to create, build and market a blog on which you create content that is of interest to both you and your readers, who can potentially become part of your small army of supporters - all of which leads to the inevitable outcome - if you're willing to work hard and passionately, you can make a living from a blog that is focused on your passion.

You have to be smart enough to use basic internet/website functionality, understand the basics and to write intelligibly, or you have to be able to pay someone who is. But outside of that, almost anyone can do this.

Your Free Gift: Lifetime Access to The Blog-Fire Method Resources Center

Inside the Blog-Fire Method Resources Center, you'll find ebooks, special reports and more, each created to help expand on the topics covered in this book - various aspects of how to make money blogging. As a way to say thank you for biying this book, I'm offering you lifetime access to this resources center at no cost. Visit the Blog-Fire Method Resources Center at
http://onlinewritingpro.com/blog-fire

Chapter 1: Blogging Basics

If you've already got a blog and it's well-established, you might not want to bother with this chapter. Here is where I'm going to explain to you exactly what a blog is and why you should consider starting one.

You'll also learn:
- How blogging about your passion can help you to earn an income
- How long it takes to start earning money from your blog
- How much time and effort you need to spend in order to make your blog successful and profitable
- How much technical knowledge you'll need to be a successful blogger

Hollywood Inspiration: Julie and Julia

Let's jump right in with an example of a blog that went insanely right. Have you see the movie *Julie and Julia* before?

The movie is the real-life story of blogging phenomenon Julie Powell, who set out to blog about her experiences cooking each of Julia Child's 524 recipes from her book *Mastering the Art of French Cooking* in just 365 days.
Her blog became so popular that she was offered a book and movie deal for her efforts. She has since published another book. While Powell's success story is one in a million, not everybody needs a book and movie deal to make a living from their blogs.

(An aside: I always enjoy inspirational movies and especially when they motivate me to get stuff going in my life. Julie and Julie is a GREAT movie to inspire you as a blogger.)

Why Powell's Idea Worked: Powell came up with a concept that was not only a challenge for herself, but one that intrigued her readers. Would she really do it? They needed to stick around and find out. And with each daily post, she proved that she'd do it.

What is a blog?

At its most basic level, a blog is an online journal. The definition according to Google is "a regularly updated website or web page, typically one run by an individual or small group, that is written in an informal or conversational style."

The word "blog" is a shortened form of the original term for this particular medium - "weblog."

Andrew Sullivan defines blogging as "…the first journalistic model that actually harnesses rather than merely exploits the true democratic nature of the web. It's a new medium finally finding a unique voice."
Meg Hourihan says a blog is "[a] collection of posts…short, informal, sometimes controversial, and sometimes deeply personal…with the freshest information at the top."

The truth is that the word "blog" is a really general statement. It can literally become almost anything you want, including the literal financial support system you've been looking for.

For the purposes of this book, we are going to go simple and define a blog as a website that you get to create and update on a regular basis.

Why should I start a blog?

I'm going to tell you everything you need to know about how to start a blog and make money from it. But first, let me tell you why creating a blog and joining the blogosphere will be worth your time.

1. Blogging is among the most popular methods being used by successful people and companies today for communicating and sharing important or useful information with their audiences.
2. Blogging offers you the opportunity to express and share your opinions, thoughts, experiences or knowledge through an uncensored platform.
3. Blogging allows you to share news, current events and trends, tutorials and more.
4. Blogging can set you up as an expert in almost any field - this alone can produce the opportunity to profit from your passion in many ways.
5. Blogging allows you to really get creative and dive into the "art" of it all, if you choose. These days, blogging allows you to go outside the box. Content might include create videos, podcasts, photo slideshows and a number of other forms of media.
6. Your blog can become a platform to not only connect with your potential customers, clients or readers, but also to figure out what they most want from you - and a place to collect a lead/potential buyers list that is so targeted it'll make your head spin.
7. Blogging offers you a way to connect with people who share your passsion.
8. You are always learning something new - and blogging offers both a vehicle for sharing that information and a tool to help you retain it; plus, if you stick to your plan to build a targeted audience, blogging can actually become your incentive to learn new things in order to teach them to your readers.

9. Blogging teaches you more about yourself, because you learn to reflect on your life, your relationships and your society in a whole new way. Plus, you will find yourself engaging intellectually with others.

10. You'll learn to argue more effectively because you'll always be looking for both sides of every story.

11. You'll become a better writer. Anything you do consistently, including writing, gets better with practice. Blogging offers a regularly scheduled opportunity to work on your craft.

12. Blogging can help you become more confident and expressive with others. That's because you learn to recognize and build your inner strength, and to build relationships with your readers. Plus, you learn that sometimes admitting your weaknesses can make for the best posts.

13. You'll learn to be brave - and you won't worry so much about making mistakes. You'll learn that, most of the time, they can be fixed - and even when they can't, they can turn out to be a blessing in disguise.

14. Blogging can help you to support people and causes that matter to you.

15. Perhaps the main reason you're here - blogging can help you to support your family financially.

How do I start a blog?

While I'll be covering each of the steps below in more detail in the following chapters, here are the basics. Please note that this is really going to be a generalized overview here - but the basic steps include the following.

1. First, choose your platform and domain name.
2. Decide whether to pay for hosting or to stick to a free platform for now.
3. Set up your site with a theme, plugins and basic design.
4. Include certain pages to optimize the user experience.
5. Set up social media accounts and build relationships.
6. Write blog posts and create images for each post.
7. Set up a series of posts before you announce the blog.

How do I make money with a blog?

There are really a ton of ways - but let's start here. For the most part, you're going to make the most money blogging by simply teaching other people what you know in a way that is easily digestible, highly useful and very actionable.

The very basic steps for any successful blogger look a lot like this.

1. Establish your home base on your blog site
2. Produce valuable content on a consistent schedule
3. Build relationships with blog readers and potential customers/clients
4. Grow your platform from the ground up (and branch out)
5. Choose, create and implement streams of income

How long should it take me to start earning money with my blog?

Unlike a lot of authors, I'm going to be straight up with you here: there are no guarantees.

Sure, I could give you examples of people who hit the bigtime within a few posts (though, to be fair, very few). I could give you examples of people who took their time to "make it" as a blogger - including myself.

But instead, I'll offer a blueprint of how to achieve real success as a blogger, as well as a detailed explanation of mistakes you can avoid along the way.

These are mistakes I either made myself, or mistakes I learned about from my fellow bloggers.

REAL TALK: If you can avoid the mistakes and if you put your efforts into the steps outlined in this book, there's no reason you couldn't be making money from your blog within 30 days - and you could be supporting your family with your blogging in as little as 60 to 90 days.

Of course, it's my job to tell you not to quit your day job before you've hit the bigtime - and it's your job to decide how "big" you need to be to consider yourself successful.

How much time do I need to spend working on my blog in order to be successful?

This is totally up to you and the speed at which you hope to achieve your success. The truth is that as bloggers, time can be our biggest challenge. We're supposed to publish a steady stream of amazing content, but in most cases, we're a one-person-show.

That means we've also got to deal with other awesome stuff, such as the following.

1. technical issues
2. regularly updating ourselves about our field/industry/niche by reading related books, blog posts and other material
3. creating new products to sell, connecting with our readers and answering their questions
4. connecting with other influencers and bloggers in our niches
5. social media marketing
6. multi-media creation and marketing
7. content marketing

The list could go on and on - but that's why we've got to be especially good at time management if we're going to make money blogging. That's why you're going to want to stick to a plan and choose your highest-value activities as your first priorities each day.

We'll discuss that concept more in the last chapter of this book, focused on how to build daily habits to become the most profitable blogger you can be.

The fact is that the more consistently you produce valuable content and the more deeply you build those relationships with your readers (and potential readers), the more quickly you can set your blog up for success.

How much technical knowledge do I need in order to build a money-making blog?

So here's the deal. Personally, I build all of my blogs myself. It's just how I roll, because I'm both a total geek and a cheapskate. When I first started blogging a decade ago, it was with next to no technical knowledge. I knew how to login to my computer, how to check email, how to follow basic instructions.

I had never started a blog before, but I managed mostly by feeling my way through it. You've already got one tool that I didn't have - me. You're going to get the benefit of my years of experience (including the things that helped take me to the next level - and which ideas to avoid) right here in this book.

Where can I find more blogging resources?

Check out my writer blog, OnlineWritingPro.com, for plenty of free resources for bloggers as well as regularly updated posts on blogging and online publishing. Plus, see the lists in this book.

Chapter 2: Choosing Your Ideal Blogging Platform

There are a wide variety of blogging platforms available. How do you know which one is right for you? Which ones can help you become most profitable?

In this chapter, we're going to cover some of the most popular platforms. We're also going to cover the following.

Which platforms I suggest and why
Which one I prefer personally
How to get started blogging at zero cost to you
When you should consider paying for hosting

What are the most popular blogging platforms?

Blogger.com
- This is usually the choice for beginners because it's the easiest one of the three to set up. Simply sign up for an account and they take you step by step through the process of getting a blog started.
- Your site comes with a free domain that contains the .blogspot domain extension.
- Of note: Blogger is affiliated with Google, so even signing up for the AdSense ads is extremely easy to do, and Blogger offers a walk-through tutorial.
- While Blogger doesn't have as many blog templates to choose from as the others do, I definitely suggest it for for those with no blogging experience who want to get launched without hassle.
- You can blog totally free here if you want. It's a great way to get your feet wet without getting too far in debt - plus you can test the water with your audience.

- It's really easy to transfer a .blogspot domain to a dedicated URL - it's a simple switch in the Blogger dashboard.
- The Blogger platform offers simple ways to transfer your content to a new platform if you ever decide to move it.

WordPress.com
- No setup costs, simple to use and no coding/technical knowledge required.
- I'd say this is for someone with slightly more techie knowledge than blogger. Wordpress.com is slightly more complicated to start a blog with, but the site does still walk you through the setting up process.
- Of course, you should take into account that there's a little more to their set up than with Blogger.
- WordPress allows you to export blogs to your domain, so marketers who've blogged a little while can move their blogs when they're comfortable doing so.
- WordPress.com stores your content for free on their servers. However, this means users receive a limited version of the WordPress software.
- WordPress offers plenty of different blog templates to choose from and many people create free templates you can download as long as the bottom of the blog gives them credit. This is perfect because when you're promoting to a niche audience, the theme can set the tone and authority of the site for the reader.
- You don't technically own your blog, so you won't have much control over ad revenue.
- Your site can be suspended by WP anytime.
- Your site must use the .wordpress extension in the name.

LiveJournal -
- If you're looking for a community-driven blog platform, this one might be for you. It offers a free account to blog with as well as a paid account option.
- Note: you do have to upgrade to a paid account to use most of LiveJournal's features.
- Ads are also a paid account benefit, so this option isn't the best choice for making money from ads with little to no start-up cost.
- Advertisers can pay you to place ads on your blog if you have a paid account.
- The free account is good for use as a networking tool to get others to visit your blog on another site where you could make money.
- Best practice? Consider LiveJournal a "feeder blog" that funnels readers through to another destination.

Tumblr
- Tumblr is community-driven, like LiveJournal, but it's pretty much free to use any of its features.
- Important to note: Tumblr has a dedicated audience who are statisically more likely to be Gen Y and Z than Gen X. This might affect whether or not you want to blog there - does that age group fit your target audience, or not?
- It's pretty easy to redirect a Tumblr blog to a dedicated URL.
- Tumblr is automatically mobile friendly and even the least technically savvy person could set it up.
- Offers unlimited storage.
- Offers up to 1k themes for free.
- Offers HTML and CSS for optimization.
- Note: backing up your blog and importing the content can be much more difficult than other platforms, and there are limited plugins.
- Monetization is difficult here.

My Preferred Blogging Platform and Why I Love It

I use WordPress.org on a private host and here's why.

- You can download the WordPress software at WordPress.org for free, and then you can upload it to your own server with private hosting.
- Personally, I prefer this option because it offers the most control and flexibility. I also love the plugins and theme variety.
- You should know that the WP on a private host option is also the one with the most technical understanding required and with the least built in support.
- However, there are plenty of ways you can get support there for very little money, such as hiring help from Fiverr for individual tasks that feel overwhelming to you.
- You could also do service exchanges with a techie friend (you edit his posts, he fixes your tech stuff up, maybe?).
- Lots of free and paid theme options available.
- Access to thousands of plugins for free.
- Search-engine friendly options.
- Warning: this platform is also most vulnerable to security threats. so be sure to secure your site.

Bottom LIne: Just Pick One and Get Started

There are many other blogging sites out there to choose from, but most offer paid accounts to utilize the best services they have.

If you ask me, going with a free account now is the best option when you want to keep costs low and earning potential high.

Remember: you can always upgrade later and get a paid account with one of the other sites.

Be sure to research those sites I mentioned (and others, if you like) to determine which one offers what you need, but don't let that get in your way. If you want to do this, you should start that blog today.

Chapter 3: Choosing a Niche

In this chapter, we're going to cover the definition of a niche and why you need to pick one. Plus, we're going to talk about the following.

- Which niche you should choose
- How to Be a Leader in Your Niche
- The Niche Blogging Blueprint
- How to choose your niche
- A list of some profitable niches
- An explanation of whether or not you really need a tight niche to succeed in today's market
- How to blog about something you don't know about
- Tips and hacks for developing your own niche

Asking the Right Questions to Find Your Niche

Asking the right questions is the most important aspect of establishing your expertise in a successful niche.

So, what does that mean, exactly?

Well, let's start with one of the niches I'm writing a lot in these days – weight loss.

Now, as someone who writes in the weight loss and fitness niche, you might have a tendency to jump ahead of your prospects and give them information on various fitness programs and weight loss maintenance.

Sure, those are major issues – but they're not the only issues.

You have got to know what to ask in order to succeed in sharing the content your readers really want.

Discovering the Right Questions to Ask

If you aren't sure what kind of questions people who are trying to lose weight might ask, get into forums on that topic and pay attention to what solutions they need. Or just start by considering the things that you, personally, have struggled with along the way in your own journey.

5 Must-Ask Questions for Every Niche

Talk to anyone you know who's facing this problem you're trying to help your reader solve - whether you do it in person or in an online forum (my favorite way). Get a feel for the issue, and then ask yourself these basic questions (regardless of the niche topic):

- What products or services does a person in this situation need or want?
- Are the immediate concerns personal or external?
- What are the emotional issues?
- What are creative, non-traditional ways to approach the problem?
- What happens next?

Do you see how these "personal impact" questions take your thinking processes beyond the usual information and typical "how to" ideas. That's because each of these questions represents a potential information product, video "how to" and affiliate product that takes a different twist than the generic options – which is exactly what you need to stand out.

You can also use the contrary approach. Kindle ebooks (non-fiction ones, anyway) tend to show what happens when the buyer follows the advice. Some viewers will read your book description on Amazon.com and dismiss it saying, "So what if I don't go that way? Maybe this advice isn't worth my time!"

But you can show them what happens by preparing a piece of pre-launch content or companion that explains the worst-case scenario or the less than ideal situation – in the case of weight loss, it'd obviously be the opposite of the benefits (weight gain, bloating, high blood pressure, diabetes, sleep apnea, etc).

And then all you've got to do is wrap up the final pages by pitching how to change this (weight loss, the dieting experience, for example) for the better with the positive spin version – aka your own method.

Thinking outside the box

You should customize your questions to your topic, of course. Need a few more ideas? Here are a few suggestions that you can use as idea starters for your ebooks and related products development.

- At what point is your reader most likely to get stuck or frustrated implementing the system you're sharing?
- What skills and ideas should your reader focus on in order to use this knowledge to move to the next level?
- What are the biggest obstacles to success for a newcomer to this system? How can you overcome them?
- How to you want your reader to feel after reading your book and trying your system?
- And the final, critically important question is: What do you want your readers to say about you or your books when they finish reading? How can you help them to find that feeling?

Want to come up with a best-selling Kindle ebook idea? Start with learning to anticipate your readers' needs and wants and write to that level. Ask the right questions! Do reader surveys.

You, Guru: How to Be a Leader in Your Niche

Every wannabe blogger has fantasies of sitting around in their PJs all day and only working for an hour a day and suddenly becoming Ariana Huffington and selling their blogs for a cool $3million, plus a $300K a year editor's job, right? Or was that just me?

The truth is that while there may be an exception to every rule, there's little chance of it going that way for the average Joe. Even Ariana Huffington had to work her ass off to get where she is.

And thanks to unethical and abusive use of automated tools and scummy spammers, search engines cracked down on that minimalist work strategy and now you have to actually make a real effort. That is actually a benefit, if you think about it, because if you want to be successful, you've got to connect directly with your audience, and once you learn to listen to them, they'll tell you exactly what they want from you.

Be Brave: The Number One Quality of a Niche Guru

You might be nervous about being a leader in your niche, but don't be. Often, when I'm coaching a blogger who feels nervous about trying to position herself as a leader or expert in her field, I hear questions and concerns like these.

- Who would want to listen to me? I'm nobody.
- There are already leaders in this niche.
- I don't have anything unique to say. Who am I to give advice?

- I'm not skinny, pretty, young, or smart enough to be a leader or guru.
- My life isn't perfect; why would I tell anyone else how to do anything?

Sure, these feelings are normal, but that doesn't mean they're accurate. I mean, look at it this way - and just for a minute, be brutally honest.

How would you like it if you only had one choice for a restaurant, a salon, a specific fashion designer, a single music style, a grocery store, etc.?

You probably wouldn't like it much, right? I know I wouldn't - I love my variety and flexibility when it comes to buying.

Keep that idea in mind! See, it works same way with leaders in a niche. Consumers connect with leaders in different ways. Some people might love a hard-ass, sarcastic, in-your-face-hard-selling individuals - and you can't fathom why - because you prefer sweet, motivating people.

The Bottom Line? Be Yourself. For Real.

The fact is that everyone's different. And whatever you have to offer, it's going to have an audience for it - your style, your voice, your message - it's unique to everyone else even if you're talking about the same niche topic.

You don't have to be an expert already. People love following along with someone on their journey from start to finish - so share where you're at and work from there.

As for looks, it's a non-issue - honestly, it does not matter one bit, so unless your purpose is to attract people with your looks, then don't worry about it. I know many bloggers who are clearly more beautiful on the inside, and the truth is that looks are fleeting anyway.

For example, a desperate mom looking for advice on parenting doesn't care if you have a crooked tooth or wrinkles under your eyes - she just needs to get some good advice on how to get her baby to sleep through the night or what to do with a picky eater. See what i mean?

Still struggling to find your niche? Try this exercise.

Take 15 minutes and write down the following categories and information in a notebook or spreadsheet.

- Jobs – What are all of the jobs you've ever had?
    - Consider things like your special training, certficates, degrees and personal experiences involved in your career – recent as well as distant past.
- Skills – In addition to any special training and career skills, you should consider personal and non-professional skills that you have,
    - What do you know or understand that people might want to learn more about? Some examples: sewing, painting, fashion, home decorating, etc.
- Hobbies & Interests – Almost anything could become a niche. In this case, if you're interested in it, chances are someone else is too.
    - Your hobbies and outside interests can also offer rich topics for best-selling ebooks, information products and more.
- People You Know –. Do you know any interesting people you could interview for your blog, or with whom you could collaborate on a particular topic? Consider this when you're thinking about defining your niche.

How to Build a Niche Blogging Blueprint

A lot of bloggers put together a blog without any real plan for how they're going to promote it or monetize it. Putting a blog together without a plan is like trying to build a house without a blueprint.

It's possible, yes. But the end result is probably going to be shoddy, and the whole thing could fall apart at any minute.

You should create a solid plan of action before you even buy the domain. You need to develop a strong blueprint before you ever get started.
Waiting until after you've already set it up and are getting traffic could mean a lot of extra work going in to correct mistakes. Changing themes and adding plugins after you're already getting traffic could interrupt your traffic. Sometimes new plugins and themes can temporarily break your blog, which could mean a loss of traffic (and money) until you're able to fix everything.

Niche Selection is Key

The first part of your plan should include choosing a niche, of course.

Do some careful market research in order to determine whether or not a niche is truly viable.
- What's your purpose for blogging?
- Do you have your own product you want to promote?
- Do you want to promote affiliate products?
- Do you want to just put AdSense or CPA offers on your site?

You need to ask yourself questions like these so that you'll know how you intend to monetize the site.

Examples of Successful Blogging Niches

- Parenting
- Finance
- Beauty
- DIY Home Dã©cor
- Fitness
- Web Design
- Social Media
- Life Coaching
- Self-Help

A Note About Affiliate Products

If you plan to promote affiliate products, you should test the products yourself before you promote them. If you don't, your visitors could end up being very upset if you promoted a product of really poor quality and they bought it because they trusted you.

Even worse, what if you end up promoting something that turns out to be a scam? You don't necessarily have to purchase every product you wish to promote.

If you can prove you have a decent amount of traffic (and sometimes if you just ask), you may be able to get free review copies of some of the products you'd like to promote. It doesn't hurt to ask.

Even if you don't have any existing traffic yet, you can write to the owner of a particular affiliate program, tell them what you're planning to do, and ask if you could get a review copy. Some people won't give you a review copy.

Plenty of marketers get requests for review copies from those who just want to get a copy of their product for free.

So if you run into a skeptic, or someone who's been burned before, you may get turned down. In this case, it's probably best to just go ahead and buy the product if you really want to promote it. If it's a scam or a really crappy product, just ask for a refund.

If you start getting a substantial amount of traffic or you get a very high PageRank in Google, you could charge a pretty penny for a link on your blog.
You can also get paid for making posts on your blog that review other sites.

Should a Blog Topic ALWAYS Be Extremely Narrow?

There are two schools of thought regarding blog topics. Some people believe your topic should be very focused, because you can bring in a flurry of laser-targeted visitors. Plus, you have less competition in smaller market segments.

Another point of view is that anything worth doing is worth doing big. They believe that the only way blogging can truly be worth it is if you're bringing in massive traffic, and the only way you can achieve that level of traffic is by being very broad – casting a wide net, so to speak.

For example, you might have a sports blog that has broad appeal. You could talk about baseball, football, basketball, soccer, tennis and golf. This would give you a much more broad appeal, and the potential for larger traffic.

But since there would be so much competition, it might take a lot longer to get more traffic coming in.

Plus, the way I see it is, if I'm interested in golf, I really won't care about the other parts of the blog, so the value of it plummets in my eyes.

But let's say you choose golf as your broad topic. Even this is broad, although you just segregated it from the other sports in existence. There are many things you could write about golf – vacations, apparel, clubs, courses, techniques, etc.

You could choose an even more targeted niche like women's golf or senior golf. This is a smaller segment of a small niche.

This means you could get traffic faster, because there would be less competition. Less competition means you have the potential to rise faster in the search engine rankings.

Of course, women's golf would get far less traffic from the number one spot of Google than the combined traffic of all of the other sports niches, but the chances of that traffic converting into a sale will soar. So basically, it boils down to how you feel about your abilities.

If you believe you have the ability to get one large blog to the top of the search engines rather quickly, then you might be able to handle a broad topic blog. If you don't believe your abilities are up to snuff, then you might want to stick with a smaller niche at first. There's no shame in it - and a blogger is an ever-evolving creature, so just go with it.

You could then link to all of your smaller blogs from your large blog. You could also start with the smaller blogs, get them to gain some popularity, and then start a large, broad blog later.

Once you start the larger blog, you'll have several smaller blogs already getting traffic and already having PR that can link to the larger blog to get it started. If you already have a lot of SEO experience and you're confident in your ability to pull off some great search engine rankings quickly, then starting with a more broad blog might be a better option.

You can still get some of the benefits of having a smaller blog by having categories for each of the smaller niches on your broad topic blog.

One last thing to keep in mind is that your traffic will be less targeted if you run a broad blog.

For example, if you have a site about skin care, you may get a lot of traffic that's just looking for information about the best lotions or skin creams. But if you start a blog about something specific, like acne, you're more likely to get people who are ready and willing to buy something.

How to Select Your Niche

Start with What You Love

First things first: you've got to be passionate about the niche; that is, assuming you plan to be the one doing the blogging. Now, if you've got an unlimited budget, you could just pay someone else to blog for you. But that will mean it'll take much longer to become profitable. Assuming you want DIY, you've got to find something that makes you passionate enough that you could talk about it anytime. That's part of the reason I'm writing this book - my passions.

For one, I like to help other people to improve their lives and to get paid to do what they love. And two, iif you get me started talking about blogging, I find it hard to shut up. That's because I love blogging, and that's why I talk about it and research it - and why I have my OnlineWritingPro.com blog. It's one of the places where I can easily talk about my passions and connect with other online writers.

Consider Your Competition

Take a look around the web and see which blogs are popular the niche you're considering. Do you think you can write better content than they can? Could you offer a different insight or angle than theirs?

Be honest with yourself - if you can't do it better or at least offer a fresh take on it, this may not be the niche for you.

The Keyword Factor

Okay, some authors will tell you that it's all about the keyword, and while there's something to the keyword factor, it's not the most important thing in the world. Even so, it's smart to consider it.

Here are a few tips that can help you use keywords to your advantage.
- Brainstorm a few topics for the niche you're considering.
- Use the ideas to create some good "long-tail keywords," which are three and four keyword phrases that are very specific to your topics and post ideas.
    - The average person will use a very specific phrase when searching the internet, and this is exactly the idea.
    - Note: the search terms keywords you personally type into your search bar should offer you some insight here.
    - There are plenty of free tools online that can help here, such as Long Tail Pro and Google's AdWords Keyword Planner.

Keyword Selection Hack: Find keywords that draw a minimum of 1,000 global searches each month; but ideally, twice that amount. To avoid drowning in a sea of competition, try not to go too far above those numbers. Go too far below and you're looking at playing to an empty theater, if you know what I mean.

Keyword Competitive Factor

- Find out if your chosen keywod is too competitive by hitting Google.com and typing in your chosen niche keyword. Then you'll be able to see how many other pages get listed in the results for the keyword, as well as any PPC (pay-per-click) competition.
- Check out the video and image results as well, just to get a feel for what the competition is doing.

Pulling the Trigger: Making Your Final Decision on Niche

Ideally, when you select your final niche, you should shoot for one that has relatively low organic competition. and one that has little paid advertisiing. A ton of PPC ads on the sidebar of the search results means that there's significant competition, and if you aren't sure you can do better, you might want to select a different niche.

Now that you've decided which niche to go with, you'll want to consider your blog title and URL. You'll want to select a domain name that matches your primary keyword if you can.

If you can't get exactly what you want, try including a few different keywords to make it work. For example, if you wanted to own a website about painting, and painting.com is taken, you could consider the following ideas for a similar SEO benefit.

- howtopaint.com
- howtostartpainting.com
- howtogetstartedinpainting.com

Chapter 4: Setting Up Your Site for Success

Now that you've chosen your platform and narrowed down your niche, you've got to set your site up for success - it's time to get that blog fire rolling!

In this chapter, we'll cover how to set your site up for success. This includes:
- Selecting and installing your theme
- Plugins you should use
- My personal list of plugins
- The importance of being "mobile-friendly" in light of Google's April 2015 updates
- A brief word about SEO (search engine optimization)

Your Theme Matters

Select and Install the Ideal Theme -- A decent theme will help to make your blog instantly appear more credible. Assuming you're not some kind of coding genius, a theme makes designing your site 100 percent easier.

Theme Hacks:
- If you're going to purchase a theme, be very picky with your money and make sure you love it. Also check out the reviews - unhappy people aren't afraid to say so. If there are problems with the theme you pick, you might want to find a similar one from a different company.
- I suggest you start with a free theme at first. Just google the name of the platform you've chosen and "free themes." Example: "Free wordpress themes" or "free blogger themes."

- Almost every blogging option offers a host of free themes within the dashboard, and that includes WordPress.org software.
- I personally keep the same basic theme on all of my sites with minor variations in order to ensure brand continuity.
- Be sure to take a look at the theme options if you can. This way, you can customize your site even further.

Plugins and Extras

Add Plugins and Extras -- While there are plenty of plugins and extras you might select to increase your chances of blogging success, many of them are platform and niche-specific. For almost every blog, the following plugins are important.

- **Google Analytics** -- a wonderful suite of site analysis tools that can help you to literally give your audience exactly what they want, as well as allowing you to see what's working on your site (and what's not) and tweak it accordingly.
- **Share Buttons** -- every blog needs a good social share plugin. It should include, at minimum, sharing to Facebook, Twitter, LinkedIn, Pinterest, StumbleUpon, Digg and Reddit. I also suggest reblogging options, such as Tumblr and Blogger, as well as email and print options.
- **An RSS Feed** -- most blogs have this built in, but if you want to customize and optimize your feed, try Google's free Feedburner service.
- **A Subscription eMail Service** -- a number of free and paid options are out there - including Google's Feedburner, Constant Contact, Aweber and my favorite, MailChimp.
- **An Email Collection Box in Your Sidebar** -- Your mailing list is so important, and your blog absolutely needs an email collection area in your sidebar, preferably in the upper left or right corner, but for mobile, up top is also useful. This can also be a menu item.

- **A Popular Posts Plugin --** This can be shockingly helpful for getting people to stick around. I have one on my site that offers different lists on different pages - some show the "all time popular" posts, while others show the currently popular posts. There are all kinds of ways to configure it
- **A Related Posts Plugin --** I use, love and recommend Zemanta for related posts, because I can add it to my browser and it instantly becomes available on almost every blogging platform. This allows me to find and select related posts from my own site as well as those around the web.
  - When I link out to my own posts, I obviously get more site traffic and lower bounce rates.
  - And when I link out to others' posts, I get more attention and they're more likely to return the favor, either by linking back or by sharing my posts with their readers via social media. It's a win-win.

Other Plugins I Personally Use
So, I think you know by now that I'm a WordPress on private hosting kind of blogger. I thought it could be helpful if I were to share with you the list of plugins I personally use on my blogs.
- **Argo Links -** Allows me to quickly link out to any story I like. Later I use the Link Roundups plugin to create link love posts - great for building on your audience and traffic.
- **Autochimp -** The plugin for my email subscription service, MailChimp. Allows people to sign up for the lists more easily and allows me to customize what I send to whom. Also makes for easier setup with autoresponders.
- **Broken Link Checker -** Sends me an email whenever it finds broken links on my site. This is very helpful for staying current and in Google's good graces. Nobody likes a broken link.
- **Click-to-Tweet -** A newer plugin for me and one that requires a bit of dedication to use regularly. But on the posts that I've managed to utilize this plugin, I have found a significant increase in traffic. I plan to go back and update many more.

- **CSV Importer** - Allows me to import zip files of content. It's a little buggy but it is the best I've found for free so far.
- **Delete Duplicate Date** - Just to make sure my site stays search-engine friendly, this little tool gives me the option to get rid of duplicate content. This may not be a problem for you if you're a new blogger - but after a decade, there are times this comes in handy for me.
- **Edit Flow** - I use this as a backup to my manual editorial calendar. It offers me a quick-look at thr content that is already scheduled and an easy ways to see any holes in my plan. It can also connect to Google Calendar, which is handy-dandy.
- **Editorial Assistant by Zemanta** - In addition to being my favorite related posts plugin, the editiorial assistant offers up royalty-free images you can use (I don't, and I'll explain why in Chapter 8), tag suggestions and link-out ideas for your text.
- **Instapage** - Allows me to quickly create landing pages that convert. Has a handy free version that is pretty useful.
- **Multi-Author Adsense** - I have this installed on my primary site because I have a few different people blogging there and each has her own Adsense account.
- **No Spam at All** - Prevents spam comments and helps to quickly manage large amounts of spam already on the site - highly suggested.
- **Paid Memberships Pro with Mailchimp Addon** - A multifaceted plugin that allows a number of customization options, such as the ability to restrict content based on a levels system. The Mailchimp Add-on adds in the ability to sync your WordPress and members quickly and consistently.
- **PopupAlly** - Allows you to create a custom pop-up for whatever you like. I use mine to collect subscribers. You could use it for a number of things. Personally, I avoided using one of these for years because the experts said it would annoy people too much. I find that with the proper settings, the benefits FAR outweigh the potential detriments. I've had zero complaints.

- **Pre-Publish Post Checklist** - This is good for new bloggers. I have it on my site because I've got a couple of newbies around. It simply reminds you of the steps you need to take to publish a proper post - and you can customize it to your site's needs.
- **Recent Tweets Widget** - Exactly what it sounds like - keeps a running RSS feed of my tweets on my site. Handy for a number of reasons.
- **Recipe Card** - This is on one of my sites because I occasionally publish recipes. It's handy and niche-specific.
- **Responsive Lightbox** - Allows users to view larger versions of the images I use in posts. And it's optimized for mobile.
- **S2 Member Framework** - A free and very powerful membership program that allows you to protect and allow content based on member roles, among other things. I use it to increase subscribers by putting my freebies in a members-only area. It works like a charm.
- **Shortcodes Ultimate** - Adds a lot of shortcode functionality to the site - very handy for an advanced blogger.
- **Simple Share Buttons Adder** - Exactly what it sounds like - lets you easily add share buttons anywhere you want.
- **Slideshow** - Makes for some easy-to-implement slideshows on your site. You can even add video.
- **Top 10** - My prefered popular posts plugin.
- **W3 Total Cache** - The highest-rated and most complete WP performance-enhancer I've found. It dramatically improves the speed and user experience of your site. It will also allow you to add browser, page, object and database caching as well as minify and content delivery network (CDN) to WordPress.
- **WordPress Importer** - Allows you to import entire WP sites to a new site.
- **WP Bouncer** - Only allows you to be logged into one device at a time. This is good for helping to combat hackers.
- **Yoast SEO** - My personal choive for an all-in-one SEO solution for WP. Includes on-page content analysis, XML silemaps and much more.

`How Important is Being Mobile-Friendly, Really?

In April of 2015, Google made waves when it announced its "mobile-friendly update." Not only did this announcement strike fear in the hearts of technically-challenged bloggers everywhere, but it also caused one of the biggest scrambles to compatibility that the industry has seen.

If you don't want to get all technical, just visit this page: https://www.google.com/webmasters/tools/mobile-friendly/ and test your site.
But if you want to know the basics on how it works, here's the deal.

Relatively speaking, mobile SEO is a new concept. As a matter of fact, research from April 2015 shows that around 59% of all small business websites here in the United states werre not mobile-compliant.

This means that if your blog and website are responsive and/or mobile-friendly, you have a decent head start over most of your online competitors. With mobile search nearing 1/4 of all searches performed by users so far this year, this could lead to a huge surge in traffic. Especially if your industry's top keyword results are filled with older sites - and I personally can attest to this one.

In the months leading up to the mobile-friendly update, Google released a number of resources outlining best practices and ways to optimize your website for mobile, mostly geared towards small and medium size businesses. Check them out here: https://developers.google.com/webmasters/mobile-sites/get-started/

If you're just getting started, just be sure to select a "responsive" or "mobile-friendly" theme and you're golden.

Beginner Blogging Design MIstakes to Avoid

1. Don't have music or video auto-loading. Not only is it a bad idea for various platforms, but realize that if someone is in a crowded place or at work, this could prove very annoying. Plus it slows down your site. You don't want to lose a reader because she didn't want to wait for your site to load!

2. Don't use a dark background with light text. It's hard to read and if a reader struggles to see the info you're trying to share, it's kind of a wash.

3. Don't use a fancy font. Stick with a basic sans serif font such as Arial. Eye-tracking studies find that many people have trouble with the curly lines of the serif fonts.

4. Don't go crazy with sidebar clutter, and don't overkill on the ads. If people struggle to FIND the info on the page, or if the messy factor makes them nervous, they'll move on quickly.

5. Don't plagarize - and that includes images. Either create your own or use royalty-free ones (this is discussed in detail in chapter 9. Not sure? Check out CopyRight.gov's fair use section: http://www.copyright.gov/fls/fl102.html.

6. Don't use "click here" as your linked keyword. A keyword phrase that is linked will not only be better for your readers, but also for the search engines.

7. Don't use a giant header. Keep it to no more than about ⅕ of your "above the fold" stuff on your desktop. Remember that you want to be mobile friendly too.

8. Don't give up your personal, sensitive info - as far as your address, your kids' real names (if that's a concern) and etc. Just be smart about what you share on a personal info level - you never know who might catch wind and use it against you.

A Brief Word on SEO

Between you, me and the tree, SEO is great and it works if you work it right. But the truth is that these days, Google's algorhitims are smarterr than your average blogger - so the best way to work this deal is to write quality content that people want to read. Then you can use your Google Analytics and other various tools mentioned earlier to help naturally increase your SEO by writing naturally-flowing posts in response to what your readers are searching for.

One of the biggest mistakes you can make is to write awkward and uncomfortable articles in order to make it fit the SEO keywords you think you should be using. Even a slightly informed reader will sense that and hit the road fast.

Chapter 5: Your Email List

In this chapter, we're going to cover the importance of your email list and how to set one up.
We'll also discuss the following.

- eMail List Provider Options
- Whether or not a popup is a good idea
- Paid vs. Free: email and list management services
- Other ways to build your list
- Tips for ethical ways to "bribe" people to subscribe.

How to Start Building Your List

Once you've chosen your niche and your platform and set up your site for success, the first thing you need to do is set up an email list. I suggest a free account with your preferred mail service to get you started, unless you're already operating a profitable business.

Mailing List Providers: You've Got Options

Personally, I love Mailchimp and it's free for up to a certain number of users (1k, I think?) but the free version has limited features. Even so, I would not pay for a service just yet if i were you, at least not until it becomes necessary OR your blog has become profitable and it's sensible to do so.

Another free option is Google's Feedburner which is simple but has plenty of great promo tools.
You might even want to go ahead and burn your feed there for RSS either way – there are some SEO benefits if you do.

Make It Easy to Subscribe to Your Blog

Once you get the list set up, set up a widget on your blog in the sidebar and/or footer, and maybe consider adding a popup which invites people to subscribe after they've been on the site for a minute or two.

That can all be done free as well – like I said before, I like the popup plugin for WordPress. If you can, also add a call-to-action in each post inviting subscribers.

Should you add a popup to your site to gain subscribers?

It's iffy and entirely your call – people often hate them, BUT I have seen a significant increase in subscribers since adding a popup at my QueenBeeing.com blog. There are studies that have proven that it's an effective, if not annoying, method.

A tip: if you use a plugin such as the one I mentioned, you have the option to only allow the popup every few visits or less when you set it up. This is far less annoying to your readers.

Free Vs. Paid eMail Delivery and List Management Services: It All Depends on Your Needs

I am all about free whenever possible – partially because I'm cheap, and partially because there are so many free options if you're willing to look for them. Why spend money when you don't have to?

Bottom Line: When you're building a blog and you want to make money, you've GOT to get your email list on track.

Expert-Level eMail List-Building Tips

- When it comes to running an effective email marketing campaign there
- are few basic rules you should follow:
- Before you begin any email marketing campaign make sure that you
- are compliant with the CAN-SPAM laws. You can find them at:
- http://www.business.ftc.gov
- Never send unsolicited e mail (spam) – always make sure that your
- recipients have opted in to receive your email messages.
- Give your readers a clear options for managing their subscription and
- unsubscribing.
- The most important part of any email marketing campaign is building a responsive mailing list.
- This list is a collection of email addresses from people in your ideal target market, people that are asking you to send them information and offers by email. Many online marketers make all of their income just by sending email messages to their opt in lists.
- Imagine how great it must feel to send out an email and in an hour or two have your inbox full of orders. It is very possible, especially when you take the time to employ basic email marketing and list building strategies.
- If you don't have a website or blog you may want to consider setting one up just for your list building campaign, especially if you want to build a big list. If setting up a site isn't for you there are other methods that you can use, you will just have to get more creative when it comes to collecting email address.
- Don't make them think or DO too much – the easier you make it to sign up, the more email addresses you will collect!

LIST HACK: If you have an existing customer base make it a top priority to get an email address from everyone that makes a purchase from you. Whether it's during the sales process or after the purchase of one of your products make sure that you ask your customers for their email address. The optimum time to do this is before the purchase is completed as part of the checkout process.

Ask First!
Always remember that your customer must give you permission to send them promotional emails. Asking them for an email address as part of the sales process does not give you permission to add them to any other mailing list or bombard them with
promotional emails.

That can lead to spam complaints and you don't want that. Still, take the opportunity to follow up with them, ask how they liked the product or service and then entice them to join your regular mailing list.

There are many ways that you can entice people to join your mailing list.

Here are a few quick ideas that you can use:
- Give them a free gift or a discount on their next purchase when they
- subscribe.
- Send them to a webpage where they can download a free ebook,
- report or software related to the product they purchased.
- Give them a chance to win a prize, by holding a free contest or
- sweepstakes for subscribers only
- Offer them free customer support and email consulting.
- Have them fill out a survey and give them a free gift as an incentive to
- complete the form.

Chapter 6: Traffic and Your Small Army

Every blogger who earns income from their blog knows that the only way you can make money is by getting and keeping the traffic coming. Without your readers, AKA your "small army" of supporters, you wouldn't be making money at all.

In this chapter, we'll cover some of the ways to get traffic on your site. We'll also discuss the following.

- What NOT to do if you want to keep your readers around
- Best practices for building your small army
- How often you should blog to ensure your traffic is steady and your readers stay interested
- Blog hacks for staying consistent and on-topic
- How and why to use autoresponders to keep your readers engaged

How to Keep Your Readers Around

So we know that there are lots of ways to get readers there, but the question is -how do you keep them around?

If a reader isn't impressed by your blog, then they'll leave your blog, never to return again.
If they're a fellow blogger, they take along their blog's traffic that you could've benefited from if they'd linked to you.

Here are some common mistakes that beginning bloggers make. If you avoid them, you'll not only make make your blog appealing enough to keep your readers coming back, but you'll also have more opportunities to earn money..

The most common mistake some bloggers make is in their blog's design. Blog readers not only look for interesting and informative content- they also want to come to an inviting space to read it.

The blog's design needs to be inviting to them and even sort of comforting.

Don't Be Annoying!

Make sure you're not annoying readers with a colored font that's hard to read or a bunch of graphics that are too distracting.

A few animated graphics are fine, but don't have flashing ads and glittering graphics detracting from your blog's message – or your strategically placed advertisements.

It's fine to use colored font for your posts, but make sure it's easy to read. A pale yellow font color against a pure white background may be too difficult for the visitors to read.

They shouldn't clash with the background color either. Clashing colors can give visitors headaches, so they'll leave your site without bookmarking it for a later visit.

Be Consistent and Relevant!

The other common mistake bloggers tend to make is with their content.

Some bloggers don't update very often. If you only post once a month, your readers will forget you're there and won't return to your site.

Blog Hack: Post to your blog at least three times a week to keep human visitors and search engine spiders coming back.

Use Multi-Media to Be Multi-Faceted

Some bloggers also make the mistake of only providing text content to their blogs. Text posts are great, but mix it up a little every once in awhile with multi-media formats.

Provide some interesting pictures, audio files and videos. Offer a little variety and your visitors will come back to check and see what else you've been up to.

Stick to Your Niche

It's also important to stick to your blog's niche topic. If you're blogging about Homeschooling, then stick to that topic. Providing information about a celebrity's latest excursion will turn off your readers unless it somehow relates to homeschooling. To make your blog successful in bringing you money, make sure you make the blog appealing to your readers. If your readers keep coming back, your chances of making money from your ads and offers will increase.

The Daily Content Grind: When, how and why

How often should I be putting new content up?
As for new content, that's entirely up to you. Just try to keep it on some kind of schedule so your readers know what to expect.

I post at least a few times a day and find that to be best for my site; however, that wasn't an overnight development. I think personally every day is necessary eventually, but everyone has a different plan – and depending on your niche and audience, it may not be necessary for you.

Help With Daily Posting
There are a couple of plugins available that can help you out with getting those posts up every day. One of my favorites is Argo Links.

It's free and it allows me to find stories I like, write my opinion and link out to it.

Then I can create a link love post almost instantly too but just doing an "Argo Links Roundup," making my life 100 percent easier, and making for instant content. Handy dandy.

Another tool I like is WhizPress, which costs around ten bucks a month. It's somewhat primitave but easy to use.

Looking for post ideas?

Link love posts (also known as "roundup posts") are awesome for both networking and for traffic. That means that you collect a series of links that all relate to a specific topic and/or various aspects of it.

If you really want to make a bang with a link love post, tweet out to each author you feature in the post. This can open up entire new audiences for you.

Another thing to consider: list posts in general are good for traffic, so if you feel like you need a quick-write blog topic, consider something like "Top 10 Ways to _____" or "27 Tips for _____."

General Posting Advice (Formatting)

People want short paragraphs, bold headlines, lots of bullet points and all of your posts should be easy to skim in general. Most people don't read the full post, but long posts also do well though especially in the long term when it comes to SEO value

Post Juice

While it'll only offer you temporary traffic for the most part, anytime you can use a celebrity name and keep it on topic, that can also help.

Like I said, it won't necessarily be high quality traffic all the time – still I throw them in weekly because they help me get exposure and every loyal reader is important.

Staying on Track With Posting

If you're human, you have the potential to miss a post now and again if you're not careful. That's why I'm so glad that you can schedule posts ahead of time to avoid missing a post – and to ensure that you're publishing at an optimal time.

How and Why to Use Auto-Responders to Personalize Your Email List

It's really simple to personalize email to your lists these days, thanks to the various mail services available – but why do some emails never get opened?

Not every buyer or reader knows about autoresponders, so giving them the sense that you created an email just for each reader can really impress them!

Top 10 Tips for Personalizing Emails With Your Auto-Responder

1. When you write each response, start with the name of a trusted friend and write as if the message was just for that friend. Then edit out the friend's name and set up the message so that your autoresponder takes over and inserts the prospect's name.
2. Personalization isn't just for emails – use it as an intro to your ezine, too: "Hi, Susan, here's some great new ideas for using the XYZ Information system that I know you'll

appreciate." Use the name that the prospect gives in the information gathering form.

3. Add the name naturally as it would occur in conversation. Internet marketers can make the mistake of over-using the name just because it's easy to insert electronically. Read the message aloud before you send it – that way, you'll be able to make changes if it doesn't sound natural to you.

4. Would you use the name that many times or does it sound phony? Yes, people love the sound of their own names, but when it's over used, the reaction is that you're being a fake and that send the buyer fleeing.

5. Avoid the marital status question. Don't add Ms, Miss or Mrs to any correspondence. For one thing, email isn't that formal. And in most cases, it's irrelevant anyway.

6. Don't forget to optimize your send times. Check your analytics and see when people are opening your emails most often, and then send them at those times. Many services, such as Constant Contact, have this function built in – LOVE that.

7. Ask for your subscriber's birthday on your signup form and then auto-send a birthday greeting each year. You can even add a special gift (such as an ebook, report or toolkit) as well as a discount on other products and services if you really want to impress them.

8. If you're already using auto-responders and some are being opened less often than others, try going back in and changing your subject lines to a higher-converting, more enticing headline.

9. Use the name when you ask for the order. Remember to be personal when you make the final pitch. What's more appealing to you: "Everyone needs this marketing package to increase sales" or " I want to see you enjoy the kind of success I've had with this product – so, Stan, are you ready to make serious money online? If you are then click here. . . .but wait, Stan, I've got one more bonus that's just what you need!"

10. Once your reader signs up for your email list, you can really make yourself stand out by sending a welcome series via your autoresponder!

Here's a Sample Basic Welcome Series Template That Works

- Within an hour of signing up (but at least 15 mins. later): Send your reader a thank you message with soft call-to-action – such as "don't forget to check out your free gift," or "click here to set up your profile."
- 2-4 days after sign-up: Promotional email featuring top products or company benefits.
- 7 days after sign-up: Personal note from company CEO/top executive with a special offer.

Keep it real, keep it personal and keep making contact with your list so that the first sale isn't the last one.

Chapter 7: What to Blog About

Like we discussed before, in order to make your blog a successful money making entity, you'll need to get traffic to it and keep them coming back. And the best way to do this is to provide the best content you can in your niche and make it interesting to your blog readers.

In this chapter, we'll cover how to keep coming up with new content for your blog, as well as the following topics.

- What people like to read
- What to blog about
- What types of content will most likely go viral
- How to format the content for maximum reader retention
- Why images matter and where to find them
- How to create original images to increase your blog's hold on the search engine
- How else you can use original images to promote your site
- Why and how to write headlines that convert

Even the most successful bloggers start to run out of their own original content to post about - it is one of the challenges of the job.

Some resort to scraping the bottom of the barrel to find things to discuss, but that ultimately loses them readers, which means less money streaming in.

How and Where to Find Amazing Blog Post Ideas

So where do you find great ideas to post about?

There are actually many different things to use to get you out of your stuck--in--a--rut mode. These may be simple techniques to use, but they can be effective if used right.

Here are some things to try the next time you get stuck for something to write about:

Follow the Trends

- Search the news sites, such as Google News, CNN, MSNBC, and FOXNEWS and see if you can find a top story that you can blog about. Instead of just linking to the story, add your own accounting of it.
- You can post about your personal feelings toward the story or ask your readers what their thoughts are on it. Just make sure the story somehow relates to your blog's topic.
- Check out your fellow bloggers' sites and see what they're blogging about – It may seem unethical, but as long as you're not stealing content, it's perfectly acceptable to see what the community is interested in. Is there a post that catches your eye? Is there something you can add to that post? A new spin you can put on it?

Media outlets always have an eye on the competition to see what others are doing – and you should, too!

Do Your Research

Do a search on the Internet for your blog's topic. See what information you can come up with concerning your niche. You may become inspired by something you've read there or you may think of some comments to post about it.

Check the video sites -

- YouTube has a bazillion different videos out there that you can add to your blog. See if you can find one that relates to your blog's topic.
- Post the video to your blog and have your readers share their thoughts on it.

Consider doing reviews -

- Reviews can be a good filler to use while you try to get inspired again. Choose some articles, websites, books or whatever you can think of that's related to your blog's topic and post a review of it.
- If it's a good review, add your affiliate link and make some money from your opinions!

Daily activities -

- Think about what happened within your day that you might be able to work into your blog.
- If your blog is about flowers and you happened to go for a walk and saw some flowers on the way, use that as your post.
- Let your readers know what kinds of flowers are seen in your neighborhood and if possible, take come pictures to add since visual stimulation enhances the reader's experience.

You can easily get back your inspiration for your blog posting if you look to other sources. They can help you come up with ideas of what you can share with your readers or they can give you a nice filler until your personal inspiration comes back.

Don't lose readers just because you've lost your blogging muse!

Chapter 8: How to Write a Viral Blog Post

The first time one of my blog posts went viral, it felt a lot like a fluke. But I did my research on that post and worked on figuring out how and why it went viral. And then I set about working on how to repeat that level of success.

What had happened is that I had found a topic that touched my readers in such a way that they felt compelled to share, comment and interact around the post and in social media forums.

People discussed it, and it was, for a long time, the top-read post on my site.

More recently, I've seen my posts go viral on the regular, and many that keep on producing visitors every single day.

The top one of all time was written in August, and at the time of this writing, has more than 18k (that's 18 THOUSAND) shares to Facebook, nearly 100k visits and thousands of tweets, Pins and other various shares.

In this case, the post is in a very specific niche, and it's one that I also sell books in literally every single day – and if you ask me, it's in great part because of the viral factor of that post.

Blueprint for Blogging Success: The Components of a Viral Blog Post

I have had several posts go viral over at QueenBeeing.com, and while you can't ever really predict how it will happen, there are certain components each viral post shares. They are as follows.

The Seduction Factor

You know how you're not supposed to judge a book by its cover? Well, I'm here to tell you that as humans, we're wired to do exactly that. And that means that we're going to judge a headline by its sexy factor.

What is a sexy headline, exactly?

It's simple: it's a headline that draws you in and nearly seduces you into clicking it. It makes you WANT IT – even if you're too busy to read that article right now, you bookmark it because you're so very into that title – it makes you want to know more.

Those are the kinds of headlines you want to write.

You've got to recognize that 99.9 percent of the people who could potentially read your article will always see the headline first. That's why a headline that almost begs to be clicked is so important.

Here are a few tips to make your headlines sexy.

Make a promise you can keep.

A headline is sort of an advertisement for your blog post, if you will. It's the first thing your reader's going to see. Start by promising them something for clicking through – and then deliver in the post.

Introduce your post.

Don't call a blog post 'Top Ten Ways to Ruin Your Life' if you're going to write about how to plant a garden. This is obviously an exaggerated example, but the fact is that trying to be very mysterious or too "clever" with your post title is going to turn people off. So be sure you let people know what you're writing about.

Expert-Level Viral Blog Post TItle Hacks

Write the title after you write the post.

Leave your posts untitled until after you write them. I do this because I write my blog post titles after the post. This allows me to write the most effective title possible since there's no question of the direction the content takes.

Use a Winning Headline Formula

There are so many "tried and true" blog post title formulas that actually work that you would be shocked. A few of my favorite headline formulas:
- Here's a Quick Way to [solve a problem]
- The Ultimate Guide to [blank]
- Now You Can Have [something desirable] [great circumstance]
- How to Survive Your First [blank]
- What Everybody Ought to Know About [blank]
- How to Permanently Stop Your [blank], Even if You've Tried Everything!
- Top 10 Ways to [Blank]

The Meat: Inside a Viral Blog Post

Once the headline draws them in, it's your job to keep them there. Start by writing on topics that make you feel passionate and inspired.

And then watch which ones appeal to your audience – which posts get the most clicks and shares? Those are the ones in which you've done something right.

Study them and see what you can do to reproduce the results. Here are a few tips to get you started.

Care about what you're covering

I have noticed that the posts that go viral most often for me are the ones that I sat down and wrote in a hurry – at least the first draft.

These are the posts that cause me to wake up in the middle of the night and type furiously into my phone before I pass out again. Or the ones that come to me while I'm in traffic and I have to voice text the idea to myself so I won't forget it later.

Connect to their emotions

The fact is that emotionally-charged content has a higher percentage of social shares and gets much more interaction than it might otherwise. This is especially true in non-technical blogs – but if you think about it, didn't you click through to this post because you felt something when you read the title?

Even excitement and curiosity count as emotions in this case. And so do less desirable feelings, such as disgust, anger and sadness.

Give them something valuable (that you could charge for)

In my case, the posts that most often go viral are those which not only connect with people on an emotional level or offer them insight into a shared experience, but also those which offer TRULY USEFUL INFORMATION.
You cannot expect to regurgitate everyone else's stuff and get results. Even if you're going to link out to another blogger's post, you need to put your own unique spin on it, and you need to offer something useful.

If you're expecting the post to go viral, you might want to give them information that you'd actually charge for – say in a book or webinar.

Don't worry that they won't want to buy from you later – the opposite has been true in my case.

The more blog posts I publish in my niche, the more books I sell. There's got to be a correlation there.

Think Positive (Posts)

Despite the fact that everybody loves a good sob story, statistics tell us that the most-often shared posts are those that are positive in nature. Then again, we all know a good rant post that went viral for whatever reason – so just feel your audience out if you're not sure.

Be Real. Be Outrageous. Be You.
Here's my final tip: if you want to go viral, expose yourself a little bit. Let your reader inside your head, and don't be afraid to be yourself.

Sometimes if you can allow yourself to be genuine, vulnerable and real, your readers won't be able to like it fast enough. And when you're a real person, who really communicates with your readers? You can't lose!

Chapter 9: Best Uses of Images and How They Increase Your Viral Potential

How and Why to Create Your Own Original Images

Create an original image and include your URL on it

I used to only use royalty-free images on my blog, until one day I read a tip somewhere that suggested that images could bring more traffic to your site.

These days, I find myself creating a custom image for each post – and I include my URL on each as well.

You can use your post's headline, or do what I do sometimes – use an alternate headline or use the pic to ask a question that makes people want to know the answer. Other times, I'll just use a powerful quote that relates to the post.

I believe the custom post photo works for a few reasons.

- I enter metadata on my site when I upload this pic. This includes an optimized title and site credit, as well as permission for distribution. This leads to the photo becoming indexed by Google.
- The photo is then a perfect way to help draw attention to your social media marketing on the post – there are stats everywhere these days telling you that pics are more often

shared than straight links on nearly every social media platform.

- When a photo is eye-catching and the headline is sexy, you've got a one-two punch that's got viral written all over it.

20 Free Online Places to Get Royalty-Free Images

Blog posts are significantly more likely to attract visitors when they use good, eye--catching images. If you can make your own images, even better.

You can take photos with your phone, even, or you can create them at a site such as iPiccy.com (my personal favorite and totally free!).

20 Creative Commons 0 (CC0) and Public Domain image sites.

1. Pixabay-- - A huge database of public domain images.
2. New Old Stock-- - Vintage photos from the public archives
3. Unsplash - --10 new high quality photos released every 10 days. Released under the CC0 license.
4. Foodie's Feed-- - High- -res food images. Free to use without attribution; however, the may not be resold.
5. Death to the Stock Photo-- - Free images for commercial use. Delivered monthly to your inbox. You do not have the right to claim these photos as your own.
6. Magdeleine-- - One free high--res photo every day (and access to a full repository of images). Use the handy filter to find images that are either public domain or require attribution.
7. Public Domain Archive - --All images are completely free for personal or commercial use, no link or attribution required. I personally use this for my latest startup Due for

some of the amazing whitepaper images that we're putting together for the big launch.

8. Good Free Photos -- Public domain images taken by the owner of the site. Offers some good location-based images.

9. Free Range Stock-- - Free high-res images, registration required. It is suggested you link back to the site and give credit to the photographer, but it isn't required. You cannot resell, distribute, or claim ownership of the images.

10. Pickup Image-- - Searchable database of public domain images.

11. Photogen-- - Free for personal or commercial use, but not suitable for resale or redistribution. 12. Gratisography-- - Free collection of amazing images taken by photographer Ryan McGuire. All photos provided under CC0.

13. Skitterphoto-- - License--free photos, free to use under CC0.

14. Life of Pix-- - High-q-uality, public domain images with no copyright restrictions.

15. Pexels-- - Searchable database of CC0 images.

16. Morgue File - --A huge repository of free photos. You're free to use the images for personal or commercial purposes, but you cannot claim ownership of them.

17. SplitShire-- - Free photos with no copyright restrictions.

18. 1 Million Free Pictures-- - Free amateur public domain images. What they sometimes lack in quality they make up for in quantity.

19. pdpics-- - Public domain images taken by their in-house team of photographers.

20. Flickr - Creative Commons-- access to all Flickr photos sorted by license.This allows you to find images under the public domain, non-commercial license, attribution license, etc. Make sure you select 'Public Domain' to find images that don't require attribution.

5 Tools I Personally Use for Staying on Track with Blogging

1. <u>Idea Growr app.</u> This is my newest find, but I'm adding it as number one because it has been such a huge help in my scatter-brained life already. So far, I'm using it mostly for the planning and idea stages on upcoming books and projects. I like that it sort of directs you through developing an idea fully, and for the "your questions" section, I'm using my own version of <u>Tim Castleman's 11 step creative system</u> for my questions. I also have just discovered that I can very easily export my ideas into both <u>Evernote</u> and Trello, both of which make me very happy. Speaking of which, let's move to the next tool.

2. <u>Evernote</u>. For blog posts and notes, thoughts, etc. Also for keeping track of bits and pieces of ideas as well as clipping articles and valuable info I want to refer back to later. Stuff like blog posts and reference lists. In fact, I've been writing this post on my phone in bits and pieces throughout the day. Where? You guessed it – in Evernote. I can do all the formatting and editing and literally just paste the post and go if I want, or I can just put my rough thoughts down and come back to it later for polishing.

3. <u>Trello</u>. So far, I'm finding Trello good for daily scheduling, repeating processes that I need to remember (publishing steps and a new revolving launch concept I'm working on, for example). Also awesome for for strategy and to do lists, which I find especially satisfying in checklist form. Also good for the <u>GTD system</u> and for keeping track of my someday list (a list of project and ideas I want to do but don't have time for right now). It's also a good way to add ideas from <u>Idea Growr</u> app once they are fleshed out so that you can take them to the next step.

4. <u>Buffer</u>. For scheduling social media. Free for up to 3 accounts and limited updates. I have the paid package and

love it, even though I hate paying for social media tools. This one is worth its cost just in the hours it saves me, though. It is a little glitchy at times, especially the Android version, but it works and makes posting my stuff across my networks much easier – plus helps me find related, interesting stuff that I both read and share on a pretty regular basis.

5. **WhizPress**. This is a sort of "alternative" for me – I use it when I am struggling with a blog post idea or if I want to cover news or a current event. It's a pretty cool way to find blog topics when you run out of ideas, and can also help you see what's trending. WhizPress is a paid service that offers up fresh blog ideas that are often good for traffic. It's about $10 a month, but it can be worth it for those who blog daily and need a little inspiration here and there.

Chapter 10: Hack Your Editorial Calendar

I like to take a three-pronged approach to blogging, and my editorial calendar has been key.

- First, I get everything organized. If you're scattered on your blog, it confuses the readers, search engine spiders – and even you.
- Then I map out a schedule for blogs. Having a deadline for yourself can benefit you and help you work towards a specific goal, not just something vague.
- Last, you want to begin creating your content – and we're going to cover three options for you to choose from – a series, an individual post, or a guest blog post (and you can mix these up – you don't have to choose from just one).

Getting Your Editorial Calendar Organized

There are two things you can do to get organized. The first is a planning calendar and the second is an editorial calendar, which is for completed work that you are doing on your blog. You can either buy a calendar or print one out from a site like this: http://www.pdfcalendar.com/monthly/.
Print one out for the current month, and possibly the next month. You can schedule it as far out as you like.
If you're like me, you'd prefer something electronic to keep up with your blog - and in this case, I have two options for you.

- First, you could just use Google Calendar. I find this one to be especially helpful when I'm planning on the fly because it syncs automatically to all of my devices.

- I've also been loving Edit Flow, which is a Wordpress plugin that offers me an editorial calendar right inside my dashboard.
- Not gonna lie - I recently bought a teacher's planner and have been using it as a moified blog editorial calendar. Love it.

Planning for Blogging Success

Regardless of which method you choose, this will become your blog planning calendar. You can use this to fill in the days with whatever you'll be blogging about (and we'll go over that shortly). This helps you plan what needs to be written, and when.

This is perfect for using yourself or for whenever you're using a freelance ghostwriter to create your blog content and you want to share it with them so that they can plan for publishing dates.

Once you have the blog posts created, you can use a different type of organizer to help you schedule them for publication.

Another free plugin, called WordPress Editorial Calendar makes this a simple drag and drop process - much like the Edit Flow plugin I mentioned in Chapter 4.

As soon as you upload a new post, you can drag the post around on your calendar to wherever you want it to be for it to go live.

This can help if you have some timely information that needs to bump a previously scheduled topic. By using a calendar plugin, you can glance quickly at your blog schedule and see where there are gaps.
The more you publish, the better – but there's an asterisk to that* *
It's only better when there's more if there's something valuable that you're sharing. In other words, don't blog just to blog.

Don't slap up meaningless content that dilutes the truly valuable blog posts you have just because someone told you to blog 3 times a day. What you ought to do is go through and develop your editorial calendars to see how much content you can conceivably create.

You'll be surprised at how many ideas you generate once you understand how to look for good blog ideas.

As far as search engine bots (spiders) are concerned, they like to see a certain amount of "freshness" in your blog.

They typically start off visiting your blog once every couple of weeks, but they narrow their visitation schedule to index your site if you blog regularly, and this looks good and helps you get content indexed faster.

Like I said before, it's also helpful to your blog subscribers if you blog frequently. If this is a topic they're interested in, then you want to be the go-to authority figure in your niche – the person they know will have continual updates and fresh information.

A daily schedule is best. Some people post several times and day, and this is great too. Don't burden yourself trying to reach that goal, though. Just be consistent. If you can only manage to post 3 times a week, then do it three times a week. However, there is such as thing as blogging too little.

When you start going weeks or months without blogging, don't expect a blog audience to stick around and become subscribers and fans of your content. In fact, they won't even know who you are!

Scheduling a Series for Your Blog

A series is a good way to keep people tuning back in for more. It works the same way on television – you tune in weekly to see what happens next after you've seen a cliffhanger or an upcoming episode snippet.

But what can you do a series on for your blog?
- Reviews make a good series. If you buy and implement a digital product, then you can go through the entire process in a series of blog posts. For example, your posts can include blogs about why you bought it and how the order and download or access process went (including s sales copy review). Then you can break down each step of your implementation process over the next several days.
- If it's a text product, do a chapter a day. If it's a video product, do a video a day. Always link to the previous and subsequent blog posts so that a new visitor who happens to land on your blog in the middle of it can find their way back to the beginning.
    - Step--by--step tutorials also make a great series for you to blog about.
    For example, let's say someone wanted to know how to start a container garden. You could go through a different topic each day, such as:
        - Planning your container gardening space
        - Picking which fruits and vegetables you want to grow in each season
        - Building your containers
        - Getting the soil just right
        - The planting process
        - Dealing with pests
        - Harvesting…etc.
- Q&A sessions with your audience work well for a series, too. Invite your subscribers to ask any questions they have – you can even schedule certain days to be "Mailbox" days where you answer audience questions.

7 More Ideas for Viral Blog Posts

If you're not doing a series but posting individual blog posts, there's a whole host of options for you! Make a list of these and try to mix it up on your blog so that you're not using the same old approach on a continual basis.

- Top tip lists make great blog posts. These are tips you gather and then blog about, explaining each one.

  - For example: 7 Ways to Fall Asleep Faster, 6 Ways to Say No to Sweets When You're on a Diet, the Top 3 Tips to Help You Save Money at the Grocery Store, etc.
  - Tips like this are easy to digest and people can usually come away knowing they've absorbed a few good nuggets, even if they didn't appreciate all of the tips you presented.

- Reviews were mentioned in the last section as far as series that you can do. But they can also be done for individual blog posts. You don't have to draw it out if it doesn't call for it – or if it's for a tangible item that you want to go over.
- Rants about a topic can generate a buzz for your blog. You don't want to be nothing more than a person who rants all of the time, but if you find something in your niche that needs to be exposed or discussed, don't be afraid to talk about it!
- Curated content is something that everyone is buzzing about in the blog world. You can use short snippets where you quote or reference something from a magazine, news site, book or other blog and launch a discussion about it on your blog.

- Usually, you'll do something like present a snippet or portion of something someone else created (not a swipe of their material, but a very small piece, with a link back to their site). Then you add your own commentary about it.
    - For example, you might be writing a blog post about hot flashes – and the Mayo Clinic has an article about it.
    - You can take a quote from that, link back to the full article, and discuss their findings.
    - Think of it like a dinner party where you say, "Oh did you hear about …" and then you add your own opinions, insights, and even disagreements about the subject matter.
- Categorized posts will help you develop content for your blog. Some people map out the categories for their blog as they go. But if you have categories ahead of time, it can help you develop content just for that purpose.
    - For example, if you ran a health blog, you could do a post on health tips for boys, girls, teens, men, women and seniors. Then you can go through your editorial calendar and say, "I haven't done anything on senior health this week, so I'll do that today!"
- Breaking news is always beneficial when blogging. Usually, this will help you see a spike in traffic because it's new and there won't be as many posts about it as there will be later.
    - Set up a Google Alert so that you get notified when news happens about certain topics. But also go out and search Google and specific news sites for breaking topics yourself.

Video and Podcasting: Alternative Content that Pops

Did you know that the second largest search engine in the world is YouTube? Yep. And it's only topped by Google (which, as you likely know, also owns YouTube).

Adding video content to your site on the regular van seriously increatse your exposure and visibility in the online world - and that can lead to increased success for you.

You can create your own videos or even just share related ones from YouTube on your blog for added traffic. Or, start your own podcast and share those posts as well.

About Guest Bloggers

Guest bloggers will often seek you out once your blog becomes a traffic hub for a particular niche. You won't want to accept everyone who requests a spot on your blog.

But you may want to use a guest blogger from time to time, as long as they continue with the purpose and direction of your own blog.

You can approach people or post blog topic jobs – sometimes you'll pay for the post and sometimes the blogger will be happy with a link back to their own site.

You can ask someone who is an authority figure in your niche to provide a guest blog post – this reflects well on you as a blogger because you're pulling in valuable resources for your own readers, which they'll appreciate greatly. Or, you can find new bloggers who are eager to get some experience under their belts. Either way, make sure the piece is suitable for your audience and don't let the topic veer off course.

Chapter 11: Social Media Savvy for Bloggers

As I have said repeatedly, social media is all about building relationships, and this is why it's an ideal platform to grow your blog audience and potentially your income.

In this chapter, we're going to cover how and why you should get involved with social media if you want to build a successful blog. Plus:
- The Importance of Social Media Relationships
- A Word on Self-Promotion
- Why and How to Share What Other Bloggers Write
- Building Your Social Media Strategy
- Scheduling and Automation
- Building Relationships

Why social networking is key for successful bloggers

Okay, the first thing you've got to realize is that as of 2014, social media is LITERALLY THE NUMBER ONE ACTIVITY that Americans do each day. This includes email and even Google. Simply put, your potential readers are hanging out on social media each day. So go where they are and learn to draw them in.
A Fast Company study found that 93 percent of marketers are using social media to promote their business, and the platforms aren't going away anytime soon.

People are obsessed with social media for a reason - and for marketers, it offers up a variety of ways to connect to their readers and potentially grow their biz. Same goes for bloggers.

Effective Self-Promotion and Social Media

When I first started blogging 10 years ago, I felt shy to share my posts with my friends and family, let alone the general public. I worried that they'd think I was not good enough or trying too hard - or maybe that they'd just judge me unfairly.

If you're there too, you've got to get over it! Try not to be too spammy with your posts - obviously you want to offer value and you don't want to ONLY post your own stuff. But don't be afraid to share - and if you're very worried about what your friends and family will think, you can always create standalone accounts for your blogs.

WIth that being said, I recommend just getting over it and sharing with everyone - you never know who your biggest supporters could be!

How to Build Your Social Media Strategy: A Step-by-Step Guide

Understand Your Target Audience

You can't be effective if you're EVERYWHERE, so the best tactic is to figure out where your target audience is primarily hanging out online and what the best ways are to reach them. Then you're going to focus your social media strategy on that primary goal.

Ask yourself:
- Are your target readers mostly male or female?
- Approximately how old are they (a range is okay)?
- Do they have kids? Are they married?
- What is their income level? Can they buy your stuff anyway?

Why You Need These Answers

These answers will help you decide where you're going to get the best return-on-investment when it comes to your time. Remember - time is money, especially when you're working on creating your own online income.

Why Facebook is the #1 Place to Promote Your Blog Posts and Products: The Stats

Facebook has nearly 1.5 BILLION active users each month, making it the market leader for social networking. And, if I'm being honest with you, I get about ⅔ of my total traffic from Facebook - significantly more visits, users, page views and conversions than from any other platform.

However, other networks are still valuable - here are a few of my own insights on Pinterest, Twitter and LinkedIn as they relate to marketing my own content and traffic to my blog.

- Pinterest visits are relatively small compared to Facebook, but per visitor, I get more average interaction and lower bounce rates.
- Most Pinterest users are women, 35 to 44 seems to be the largest demographic. A lot of moms and a lot of DIYers. So consider this as it applies to your niche.
- Twitter visits might produce a lot of traffic, but a lot of it is one-off traffic (and that's why the mailing list is so important).
- If you actively foster relationships on Twitter, your conversion rates will be higher.
- LinkedIn is a good place to market B2B type stuff and professional development-type content.
- LinkedIn is also a great way to connect to other professionals in your niche and related fields.

Facebook Demographics

The company data shows that the 18–24 age range is still the biggest demographic using the site.
- 87% of adults 18–29 use Facebook.
- 73% of adults 30–49 use Facebook.
- 63% of adults 50–64 use Facebook.
- 56% of adults 65+ use Facebook.

Facebook also seems to be a bit more populated with women, with 77% of adult females on the site and 66% adult males.

Also of interest - the following U.S.-based Facebook statistics

- 72% of adults living in the suburbs use Facebook.
- 71% of adults living in urban areas use Facebook.
- 69% of adults living in rural areas use Facebook.
- 71% of adults with some college experience use Facebook.
- 70% of adults who graduated high school or less use Facebook.
- 77% of adults who make less than $30,000 use Facebook.
- 74% of adults who make between $50,000-$74,999 use Facebook.
- 72% of adults who make over $75,000 use Facebook.
- 69% of adults who make between $30,000–$49,000 use Facebook.

How to Be Accessible to Your Audience

Accessibility is important to your prospects and customers. So few marketers are truly open to hearing from their customers and when it happens, word spreads and you cultivate the right kind of reputation.

Many marketers put up a wall between themselves and their online audience. They don't engage in blog comment discussions once a post is created. Even Seth Godin himself doesn't even allow comments on his blog anymore - and he's always talking about developing a loyal tribe.

So it's good to see marketers who are there for their audience and who take time to interact with the people who need and want their help. There are even some marketers who create a help desk so that tickets are opened, rather than a simple email sent.

On your blog's contact page, be sure you offer a variety of ways to get in touch with you.

- Post your email (or that of your customer service center) and a phone number or SKPYE name. If you are the "Customer service center," send those emails to a designated email box and answer them promptly.
- Add a list of all of your social media profiles and ways to connect with you there.
- Don't bother with a traditional contact form - most people won't use them anyway these days.

If you can't, at least set up an auto-responder saying that you received the customer's email and are working on the solution.

The more ways you can be contacted, the more the customer feels at ease that you aren't hiding in some unreachable corner of cyberspace.

You can't shake hands with your online customer, but you can create an ongoing buying relationship by showing them that you really are all about paying it forward and helping them out.
Of course that's an option for you, and it might even be necessary if you have a lot of technique elements to your site, but it means a lot when your reader can just contact you - and get a response from you, not a virtual assistant that you've hired - or worse - made up to make it look like you're more important than you really are (it happens).

The best way to be accessible as a leader in your niche is to do the following:

- Respond to people on social networks like Twitter, G+, Pinterest and Facebook.
- Respond to blog comments whenever you go in to approve them.
- Reply personally to your emails.
- Open comments up on things like YouTube videos to show you care about feedback.

All of these things take time, yes. But that's where you can really put a personal touch on your usually sterile online business. Going the extra mile can serve you well as a niche leader. It shows you care.

You don't have to incorporate all of these elements in one day. It will take some time to integrate them all into your business, and you may have to outsource in some other areas to free up some of your time.

Stay on top of your socialization and personalization and it makes it less overwhelming. Don't take a lot of time with it, just do it and move on without stalling and getting mired down in lengthy discussions every single time. Acknowledgement is all some people will need - to know that they've been heard and appreciated.

Bottom line: If you really want to develop a rapport with readers in a virtual environment, bloggers have got to establish trust and if you're selling stuff, do it with a money-back guarantees plus fast delivery.

Expert-Level Social Media Marketing and Networking Hacks for Bloggers

Share Others' Content if It's Useful or Interesting to Your Audience.

No matter what niche you're in, there's news that needs to be shared. There are new:

- Breakthroughs
- Trends
- Strategies
- Products
- People

So, the deal is that you've got to provide ongoing value to your readers if you want to keep them around - so you're going to want to share all the latest and greatest in your niche with your target audience.
This includes even your competitors. Personally, I don't believe there's really such a thing as competition on the internet, and we'll talk about that more in the next section.

If you are covering the anti-aging niche, for example, you might share news about a medical breakthrough that helps plump up crow's feet.

Or maybe you'll find a news story about how women are flocking to plastic surgeons to get rid of their "Madonna Mitts" - which is what I hear the iindustry calls her aging hands.

You can share things like which anti aging treatments people can do at home that you've tried and feel work best. Stay abreast of top manufacturers' or sellers' product releases and then talk to your audience about it.

Why Content Curation Works So Effectively in Social Media

Your blog or your email subscriber list will be the place where your subscriber feels they can go to gather all of the information they want. They don't want to have to go all over the Internet and buy a bunch of different products to see what works best - that's what they'll love you for!

Whenever you blog about something with a cutting edge slant to it, you increase your worth in the niche. Your readers will bookmark and share your site with others, they'll trust your recommendations whenever you want to promote something, too.

The lazy (unsuccessful) marketer does nothing but look at keyword volume, outsource their content to ghostwriters without injecting any of their own personality, and basically copycats the true leaders who are out there working for their audience the way they should be.

How and Why to Align Yourself with the Best People

When you're a true leader, you're never running solo the entire time you spend growing an online business. The top marketers understand that you work individually, but you stay connected with a team of like-minded leaders on the 'net.

Don't be afraid of your competition - embrace them. They can be guest bloggers or invite you to guest blog on their site, they can co-create products with you, and they can cross-promote you whenever you sign up as an affiliate to promote one of their products.

Don't just look to people who are bigger in status than you are, either. You want to keep an eye out for rising stars in your niche and help make them well-known, too.

It's not just competitors who you should align yourself with, either. It's anyone whose products or services are related to your own niche in some way. Let's go through an example.

A Sample Online Netwoking Strategy for Bloggers

Let's say that you run a diet blog that teaches people how to embrace a healthy lifestyle through nutrition. You want people to adopt life long eating habits that improve their lives.

You can certainly promote other leaders in the diet niche - like someone specializing in juicing, for example - but you also want to connect with someone whose information is relevant, if not directly identical.

An exercise and fitness leader would be a good example of this. People learning about good nutrition often want the whole body approach, which means moving your body and getting fit.

So, as a diet blogger, you also might want to align with the following kinds of bloggers and influencers.
- An influential parenting blogger so you can help their audience learn about good nutrition for growing kids.
- A well-known aging leader so you can teach good nutrition for senior citizens.
- A highly-respected job success coach so you can offer information about staying alert and energetic during a long workday.
- A local journalist who has a history of covering health-related stories

See? There are endless possibilities for someone if you think about the target audience who needs what you teach and then consider who else they might be learning from. Here are some more examples that relate to other nihes.

- A smoking cessation leader so you can help smokers quit their bad habit without gaining a lot of weight.
- An Amazon affiliate who runs a site about desserts so you can provide information on healthier dessert options.
- A skincare leader so you can teach good nutrition that helps your skin maintain its youth and appeal.

Make a list and then make it a point to reach out to those other leaders and form a bond with them so that you can help each other out as you both grow your online business.

A Word About Social Bookmarking

Social bookmarking is, for all intents and purposes, the electronic version of leaving a breadcrumb trail. So, why not get your Hansel and Gretel on?
But how does social bookmarking benefit you as a blogger who is trying to make money?

Consider this: you can have a great product, but without enough traffic, it's just another "nothing" on the 'net.

Even if you have a faithful readership and an overflowing email list, if you're going to make any real money with your blog in the long run, you constantly need to be reaching new online viewers.

The good news? The options for connecting with social bookmarkers are exploding right now.

That's why you need to surf around and see what's out there, then set up a series of "regular" social bookmarking accounts to use.

A few examples:

- **StumbleUpon is one of the leading social bookmarking sites that's both easy to use and powerful.** Once you create an account, you can add the toolbar interface. Then all you do is click the Thumbs Up icon to recommend a site. You can do this for your own sites, or ask your friends to submit a Thumbs Up rating for you. Besides the rating, you can add comments about the site. Personally, I get a small amount of traffic from StumbleUpon and the conversion rate is similar to other sources.
- **Can y'all Digg it?** It's not just a line from some old 70s movie - it's also a widely used social bookmarking site. Digg functions much like Stumble Upon with raters given the chance push the ratings of a site to the front page. Making it to the front page of Digg gets your information in front of thousands of viewers and it helps traffic flood in to read your newsworthy submission.
- **Try Climmarks!** Clipmarks describes itself as "scissors for web pages." As with other social bookmarking sites, you can submit items that are sent to the web - including to Facebook or to an iPhone. As a one stop service and huge time saver, sign up with OnlyWire. Personally, I don't use this one.
- **The Reddit Cult.** I hesitate to list Reddit here, because it's so much more than a bookmarking site. But if you can get the Redditors to look at your stuff and recommend it, your life could change after the traffic hits your site.

Tips for bookmarking from your blog

- Make it easy for your readers to bookmark your content. You begin by installing a plugin for your browser, and then you only need a single click to submit your item to multiple sites.
- To make this work, you still need to sign up at bookmarking sites that you plan to use. After that, you can use OnlyWire to handle the multiple submissions.

- Make sure your site viewers know how to rate your site. You can't reward or bribe them for bookmarking your site. That's the social bookmarking version of stuffing the ballot box at voting time.
- You can put links to the bookmarking sites on your sites as a gentle reminder.
- Don't be shy about submitting your new information to the networks yourself – just make sure you also submit other sites so that you don't appear spammy.
- Let people know what you've got and where to find your site and they'll share that information with others.

Karma is a Bitch: How to Promote and Produce with Ethics in Mind

I don't care what you believe in - there's something to be said for the concept of karma and how when you do good in the wold, more of it comes back to you. The same can be said for making money online - if you're going to do it and expect to make a living of it, you've got to keep it all above board, and that means keeping your readers in mind.

A substandard product will cause your readers to lose trust in you, and that means they won't be your readers for long. In today's market, the most successful bloggers give away their best stuff - just look at Chris Brogan, Neil Patel and Darren Rowse if you don't believe me.

That's why you've got to do your very best to avoid creating or promoting products that you personally would not pay for. Never create products where you intend to leave vital information out or intentionally mislead your target audience. People who market products based on trends or fads alone often do it without even considering whether or not it's the right thing to do.

They're after only one thing - money.

You know it. I know it. And everybody knows it.

So please. Hear me now and take heed: when you create products, don't do what some online experts do and leave crucial details out of the product - in an attempt to squeeze more money out of your target audience at a later date.

Here's a good example:

Let's say you're a blogging expert. Maybe you put out a product that teaches someone how to blog. But your blog product only covers the topics like finding what to blog about, how often to blog, engaging your customers.

All of this is good information, of course - but you left out a very important part of the puzzle - how to set up the blog in the first place! This kind of behavior isn't always intentional.

You might have truly forgotten that the reader doesn't even know how to buy a domain name, get hosting, and install a blog because you're well past that stage. Still, it's your responsibility as a good leader to provide that for them.

Don't leave it out so you can sell it as separate information in another course, or as an upsell or one time offer. That's not the attitude of a true leader - that's the attitude of a freaking scrub Don't be a scrub, my friend.

What if you accidentally leave out vital informmation?

Listen, nobody is perfect, and it's possible that you accidentally left out someting important in your product. If that's the case, and you get a comment from a user about it, then you can actually use this to your advantage. It can help you build relationships.

All you need to do is send out an email to everyone who has already purchased the product and give them the additional information free. Then, you update your product and promote the new and improved version to new readers as well.

This will help your existing readers to learn that not only do you genuinely want to help them, but that you really care about how they see your work and that you want it to be valuable to them. These are irresistable qualities in anyone who's asking ME to spend MY money. How about you?

Chapter 12: Making Money With Your Blog

Making money online is very different than more traditional methods, but there are certain things that remain consistent. One of those things is the psychology of what makes people spend their money online.

In this chapter, we're going to look at that psychology and how we can tap into it in order to sell more products through our blogs. We're also going to talk about the following.
How the internet changed the way people buy
How eBay changed the world
How to apply the psychology of eBay buying to your blog products
The ABCs of Buying
Proven ways to make more money with your blog

A Psychology Primer: Why People Spend Money Online

If you're breathing these days, you already know that online shopping is no longer the exception - it's a major share of business, even for the massive discount stores with a strong retail presence. With the improvements in secure transactions for credit card information, more buyers of all ages feel safe shopping online.

If you're a solo blogger and not a brand name business, what makes people want to buy from you? The answer is the same regardless of the size of the business and even the nature of the product.

It's all about the psychology of online spending - almost more than even the product itself or the price you're charging.

The Internet is offers the most unique vehicle for connection in the known history of the world. Nope, I' not exaggerating even a bit.

Before the internet, there was television. And before that, movies in various iterations. But the internet does something that no other medium has done before - offers you the ability to have real-time interaction with your potential buyers from the comfort of your separate worlds.

This makes the internet sort of huge and personal at the same time. Your prospects aren't riding along the Internet the way they ride on a subway. Your prospects their own online experiences with their interests, searches, desires and purchases.

Trends on the Internet are people-driven. Your site may be seen all over the world, but it still needs to be tightly focused to appeal to your best prospects.

You can't create a one-size-fits-all site, so make sure that you don't confuse prospects by being too all encompassing.

First Impressions DO Matter Online

Put the virtual welcome map out for prospects by making them feel comfortable at your site. Excitement drives purchases online. If you've bid on an item on eBay, chances are you've been caught up in the online auction wars.

How eBay Changed the Face of Online Buying

If you've never heard of eBay, chances are you're not even reading this book. eBay is a household name because it changed the way the world buys things.

Just like a live auction, the eBay-style online auction creates that desperation among buyers who want to get the item partly because they want it but also to win the item from other bidders.

It's envy personified.

The Blogger's Version: Scarcity and How to Use It to Your Advantage

You don't need an auction to create a buying frenzy. You can do that with a limited number of products or a limited time special offer.

That off the list stuff you toss in your grocery cart while waiting to check out are impulse buys. Retailers know that this is the last chance to get you to buy things that you don't need just because it's there and appears to be a bargain.

The bonus products at the end of the sales letter are the online version of the impulse buy.

You might resist the major product only to be hooked by the extra offers. When it comes down to what makes people buy online, the reasons are the same for buying a $17 information product as for buying a $17,000 painting at a local fine arts gallery.

An Easy-to-Remember Formula for Creating Info Products: The ABCs of Buying Psychology

Acquire – thee need to feel as though we have more, better and/or flashier stuff than our friends, neighbors or colleagues
Better – the desire to own or understand the most trendy, new item or improved version of the item
Convenience – the desire to have something to make your life easier, more comfortable (this one works well for info products)
Distraction – something that offers the user/buyer a way to check out of the mundane aspects of life and live in the fantasy world for even a short time
Envy – the natural urge to create envy among others because you have the first, best or most exclusive product

So the bottom line is that it's about both understanding who your target market is, as well as understanding WHY they want that product. How does it appeal to them? What makes them want it so badly and how can you tap into that and get them what they want, while making money doing what you love?

This is what the ABCs will do. So when you're creating your products or selecting your endorsements, always check the ABCs and keep that focus on your presentation.

How to Build and Inventory Your Information Products

One attraction for an online business that sells information is that your car can still fit into the garage. If you were selling tangibles on a site like eBay, your car would be out in the rain because the garage would be filled with inventory.

That's both costly and inconvenient. With online marketing of information, your "inventory" of products can fit on the thumb drive in your pocket. Even if you sell actual deliverable products, you can have those sent from a reseller and have plenty of room at home.

Since your products don't take up space, it's easy to forget just how many "assets" your business owns. You need to keep an ongoing list of the "assets" for your Internet marketing efforts. Not only do these have an economic value, but you want to know what's available and have it organized for your convenience.

It's too easy for files to get lost on the hard drive and linger instead of getting revised and back on the market. Keep everything in separate folders or files and then make a back-up on a regular basis. It only takes on computer meltdown to lose your entire business in a flash.

Some of your online assets that will help you make more money include the following.

- EBooks – custom written, original product or collaboration.
- PLR Products – articles, eBooks or courses that you own rights to resell
- Articles and reviews related to your niche
- Video or audio products that are marketed separately or with eBooks
- Product reviews and testimonials from satisfied buyers
- Recommendations from influential people in your niche market
- Sales letters, squeeze page copy and ad copy from successful campaigns
- Graphics and logos identifiable as the "brand" for your site
- Opt-in pages and forms from successful campaigns

As standalone products, these "assets" have a monetary value, but just like everything else - they're nothing until you "monetize" them for online marketing.

A few more helpful tips:

- You want to position your product as user friendly and open for refund. Granted, this is easier with downloads and information products than with shipped products.
- But even shipped products that offer guaranteed, no questions asked refunds actually have fewer refunds because the consumer feels free to try to return it if they're not satisfied. Before the sale, you want to provide ample information about the product - including several photo views if appropriate.
- Think about the questions a buyer might ask and have the answers ready before the question arrives. An easy way to provide this information is with an expanded FAQ (frequently asked questions) page. Make sure there's a link to the FAQ page from each product page.

- If your product requires assembly after delivery, post an extra copy of how to assemble it. Even better is to post a video showing and telling how to do the assembly. Another great idea is to post videos showing alternative ways to use the product. This gives buyers options that they might not have considered.

From Reader to Buyer: Expert-Level Conversion Hacks for Bloggers

Scare the money out of 'em. Ethically, of course. Sure it's great that a viewer wants your product, but desire isn't as strong as fear. Make your sales copy emphasize the scarcity of the product and how terrible it would be to miss out.

For example, if you're trying to sell your custom website design services, you might use the following kind of copy.

"You could spend many frustrated hours trying to make those purchased templates look like a custom website - but you're stuck with a few colors and choices and few easy-to-customize options. Meanwhile, marketers with XYZ Web Page SuperDuper Gold Package are up and running in an hour with the look of expensive graphics."

Why this works: because this will cause your reader to picture the competition making money while he's still fighting with fonts. That's fear – fear of being left out.

Only be wordy if you can keep 'em hooked. Long sales copy works only if it's not boring. In an effort to create the typical long sales letter, inexperienced writers just repeat the same information with little variation. This isn't the time to "do it yourself."
Really successful bloggers know how to get that same information across in fresh ways so that each section of the sales letter is

familiar, yet not repetitious. If you don't have the skill do to that, then hire a professional copywriter.

If you can't afford a high-end copywriter, do your homework and hire a good one from Fiverr.com. What you pay for a good sales letter is a direct investment in traffic conversion - and it'll work better than you'd believe.

That's why you ought to just suck it up and consider it a one-time expense for endless traffic conversion opportunities.

Go against your gut, just this one time, and raise the price. Look, you don't need to start typing up your email to complain about how crazy I am. I already know what you're thinking.

"But wait, if sales are falling, why would charging more be better? That seems counterintuitive!"

You're right, it does. But the truth is that maybe you may have under-priced your product, which gives it a lower value in a lot of people's minds.

Worried that it's not worth the jump in price? Then you've got something to worry about. o something to make it more attractive and valuable. Here are a few ideas.

- Add another section or package with a second information product.
- Create a companion product or giveaway.
- Shoot a series of videos and offer them free with your product.
- Change the cover design.
- Add new delivery options so that a buyer can choose eBook, CD or MP3 audio product formats.

These small changes give you a reason to bump up the price. And don't be a baby and only bump your price from $9.95 to $12.95. BE BOLD! Take the price up to $17 or $27 and hype the promotion.

The Art of the Limited-Time Offer

If you really want to create a sense of urgency and make a lot of money fast, try this one. Once you've got a relatively active group of reades, try a limited-time offer.

It really is an art form.

Here's a simple example of a limited time discount - "Order now to get the product for $12.95 because in 48 hours, the price goes to $17!"

Key Tips on How to Make an Effective Limited Time Offer.
- Create urgency by offering a one time purchase to a limited number of buyers for a short time. This plays to fear ("what if I miss it?") and scarcity ("I want it before someone else gets it").
- IMPORTANT! You've got to follow through with what you say - if the offer is limited time, then make that the deal.
- DO NOT FAIL to take the product off the market at the end of the offer or to raise the price as promised.
- Remember: Nothing discredits you more than repeated "limited time" runs.
- Remove the product, make a few changes or updates and add something else to the package. Then - and only then - can you bring back the product without losing face and buyers.

Chapter 13: Your Ultimate Guide to In-Person Marketing for Bloggers

So, if you're like me, you do most of your work solo – and when you do work with collaborators, you do so virtually for the most part. And sometimes, that's enough.

But when you're ready to take your work to the next level, or if you're working primarily a local beat, you might want to get involved in some in-person networking events.

How does in-person networking make you feel?

Since a lot of online writers work from home, in-person networking events might feel a little more stressful than they would for someone who's already working "out in the world" every day.
That's why, if you're going to do this successfully, you've got to be honest with yourself and figure out your challenges in advance.

Ask yourself: Are you nervous when you think about these kinds of things?
1. Do your palms start sweating and your heart start pounding when you think about it? Do you start stressing so hard about what to wear that you get a pimple at the most inopportune time?
2. Can preparation make a difference in the way you feel?
3. Could it make a difference in the actual results of the event?
4. Maybe you feel confident tweaking your LinkedIn profile, but you'd rather cut off your left arm than think about building connections face to face?
5. If you are at-ease in most social situations, does the idea of trying to "sell yourself" make you nervous?

If you're human, there is probably at least one thing on that list you can identify with. But don't worry, my socially-challenged friend. I've got you covered – keep reading. I'm sharing my comprehensive step-by-step plan for in-person networking event success – and I'm starting with the PRE-EVENT part.

Dazzle Time: Here's Your Step-by-Step In-Networking Success Blueprint

With a little advance planning and positive thinking, you can be just as poised at networking events as you are behind your computer screen. Try these suggestions for working a room and dazzling at any event.

Pre-event networking tips: What to do before the day of the event

1. Know before you go! Do your research. Advance research is a great solution whenever you want to calm your nerves and make a strong impression. Browse online for details about the event, venue, and expected crowd.
2. Get clear first. Clarify your purpose. Focus on your goals instead of the butterflies in your stomach. Maybe you want to invite two new acquaintances out for coffee. Maybe you want to consult with experts about the impact of recent legislation on your industry.
3. Invite a plus one. Bring a friend. While you eventually want to be able to muster the courage to fly solo, companionship can help while you're still in training. Just be sure to split up frequently so you can mingle with others.

4. Offer to help – free. Volunteer your services. Transform yourself into an instant insider. Call the hosts and offer to help with registration or escorting speakers. You'll probably meet more participants, and your role provides an instant icebreaker as guests come to you for information.

5. Be dazzling! Prepare small talk. Are you stumped for something to say? Read up on breaking industry news. Write down questions you want to discuss with other guests. If appropriate, practice a couple of jokes or interesting stories to share. It may seem like overdoing it, but if you're prepared, you can truly seem more at ease and it'll be more beneficial for any professional relationships you can form.

6. Plan ahead to dress the part. Appearances count too. Convey that you have a lot in common by going along with the dress code for suits and ties, or polo shirts and khakis. You'll feel more at ease and start to build rapport.

7. Don't forget to bring mints. Smell as good as you look. Fresh breath makes it easier to wow others with what you have to say.

What Successful Bloggers Need to Bring to a Networking Event

For bloggers, there could be a variety of reasons you'd attend a networking event.

- Maybe you are looking for new freelance clients or you want to write a story about the event.
- Maybe you've got a local news blog, and you're looking for a sponsor – or maybe you're an online marketing professional looking for companies to sign on with your agency.

Regardless of the reason, bring along a few different things to make prospects remember you and follow up.

1. **Business cards** – you should have, at the very least, your name, phone number, email address and URL. I also like to include a list of services offered and/or a link to my book (which is a handy and easy-to-remember redirect to my Amazon author page - BooksAngieWrote.com).
2. **A tablet connected to a wireless provider (your cell phone company)** – with a tablet, your possibilities are endless. For an online writer, you could use it to show your work to prospects, including blogs, videos, online articles and social media pages you've built, among other things. But you could also use it to collect email addresses for people who want to sign up for a list and for doing demonstrations on various tools and techniques you might be working on or with.
3. **An interesting giveaway** – maybe a physical coupon with an ebook coupon code for download, or a cool pen, or any number of swag items available for next to nothing around the internet. A little notebook, chapstick or a small stack of sticky notes – look at sites like VistaPrint and CafePress for more ideas – both are reasonably priced and I've used both (so I can tell you they're legit). The one thing that you need to do is make sure it has your name and URL on it – and maybe a tagline to remind the user what you do, if it's not obvious by the name on the item. Everybody loves free, useful stuff. While you'll only get maybe one out of 50 giveaways to pay off, it can still turn out to be worth the trouble in referrals and even the actual ROI in the long run.

Go Time: What to Do During Your Networking Events

1. GLOW! Radiate enthusiasm. Smile wide and think positive. Remember how beneficial the event can be for your career and how much you appreciate those around you.

2. Have a winning posture. Straighten up. Good posture boosts your mood and shows others that you're strong and capable. Tuck your stomach in and roll your shoulders back and down.

3. Keep your eye on the prize. And make eye contact. Starting conversations with strangers can be challenging. Establishing eye contact is a natural way to gain someone's attention and introduce yourself. From there, you can start chatting about the food or the program.

4. Make them want you – here's how. Express interest. Guests at a networking event are likely to be eager to talk about themselves and their business. Ask open-ended questions that keep the conversation going. Share your own relevant experiences, and make sure to be relaxed – don't try to close any deals during a networking event. Just focus on relationships and if you find someone you want to do business with, exchange information and make arrangements to meet later.

5. Don't be fake! Be authentically yourself – even though you've practiced ahead of time. There's plenty of advice available about networking. Sift through the information for tips that match your strengths and personality – remember that being honest will make future connections and business relationships more smooth. Never pretend to be something you're not – it'll just cause you and everyone else frustration later.

6. Do be selective! Slow down. Pace yourself. Be courteous and friendly to each guest, but reserve your business cards for those colleagues you're interested in following up with. Enjoy your initial conversations without rushing to connect on social media or promote your own products and services. Healthy relationships are based on trust that grows over time.
7. Keep moving! Don't stay in one conversation or one place for long. Leave your contacts wanting more. Like I said, it's usually more productive to strike up brief conversations and make plans to talk again later if you think you've discovered a potential client or partner. That way you can dial down the pressure and explore more options.

Grind on: What to do after the event

1. Follow up with prospects. If you've connected with new people, shoot them an email or make a call to set up a lunch or coffee meeting to discuss the next step in your potential partnership.
2. Revisit the event in your mind and think about what you could've done better. Then make the changes during the next event to fine-tune your approach.
3. Start preparing for the next event!

Using this basic networking success plan, you can now show up at annual conventions and monthly luncheons ready to make new contacts and stay in touch with old friends.
And you can do it with ease, style and grace. What could be better? Remember, you create business and social opportunities by reaching out to others. Allow your real self to shine through and feel your new-found confidence – and nothing will stand in the way of your success. Are you ready?

About the Author

Angela Atkinson is a journalist and professional blogger who also happens to be a Certified Life Coach. See other books she has published at BooksAngieWrote.com.

Along with her solution-focused life coaching experience, Atkinson's love of writing offers her the unique ability to share a new understanding of how life works for a whole new generation.

Atkinson's publishing resume is vast and varied and includes several years' experience in online journalism, including hard reporting as well as functioning as an editor in various iterations over the years.

In her life coaching practice, Atkinson's clients enjoy her personalized approach that allows and encourages them to become the best possible versions of themselves and to succeed in doing what they love most.

Atkinson is also a relationship coach and a recognized expert on narcissism and narcissistic personality disorder. She has studied and written extensively on narcissistic relationships, as well as having survived several of her own.

As you can see when you visit the freebies page at QueenBeeing.com, Atkinson's online daily magazine for women, she's all about paying it forward. She also blogs at OnlineWritingPro.com. See the most updated list of her published books at BooksAngieWrote.com.

Professional Affiliations

Atkinson is a member of the Society of Professional Journalists, including the St. Louis Pro Chapter and the national organization. She is also a a member of the Universal Coach Institute alumni, the St. Louis Writers Guild, the National Education Writers Association and the Freelancers Union. She studied journalism at Eastern Illinois University and earned her life coach certification through the Universal Coach Institute.

Get in Touch with Angie

Here are some ways we can connect:
- Email (angyatkinson@gmail.com)
- Twitter (@angieatkinson)
- Facebook
- LinkedIn
- Google +
- Pinterest
https://www.pinterest.com/angyatkinson/

www.ingramcontent.com/pod-product-compliance
Lightning Source LLC
Chambersburg PA
CBHW070827180526
45168CB00002B/760